Questions?

about love & other mysteries

THOMAS TIMMINS

Copyright © 2021 Thomas Timmins
All rights reserved.

Printed in the United States of America

ISBN 978-1-7366334-1-0

Published by Zoëtown® Media
Zoëtown is registered trademark of Zoëtown Media.
Greenfield, MA

www.thomastimmins.com

Book and Cover Design by Maureen Moore
Booksmyth Press, Shelburne Falls, MA

Dedication

To my children and their children for asking "Why," forcing me to come up with a story or a metaphor or a fact or another question so we could learn together.

To the memory of Richard Feynman who questioned everything, even "irrefutable" scientific truth of his own discovery.

Contents

Nature	17
Society	38
Philosophy & Art	74
Science	98
Self & Relationships	113
Family	136
Agency	146
Love	177
Credits	191

I wonder, wonder who,
who mmm b'dodo, who
Who wrote the Book of Love?
Baby, baby, baby,
Tell me, tell me, tell me
O who wrote the Book of Love?

—Lindsey Buckingham/Richard Dashut,
The Monotones recording

It is the responsibility of every scientist to leave the world with more questions than answers.

—Natalie Batalha
The astronomer who spearheaded NASA's *Kepler* mission and its search for habitable worlds beyond our solar system.

How can we live without
the unknown before us?

—*Rene Char*

The curious are always in some danger.
If you are curious you might
never come home.

—Jeanette Winterson

> I wonder wonder why
> ba dydydy
> why?
>
> —*Dion and the Belmonds*

> Who put the bomp ina
> bompshebomp shebomp
> Who put the ring ina
> ringy ding ding dang
>
> —*Barry Mann*

Nature

In the spring garden, where the mulch
lies thick will roses bloom or tulips?

Do the stones in abandoned fields have
memories of cows and sheep?

Did you notice the stoop in Brooklyn blooming
with children's laughs?

Do you work harder than a fern works
when it waves in the breeze?

Does an outburst of bluettes remind you
of a valley or a mountain?

Does a virus bloom like a flower inside the
body's garden?

Are you more like a tree
than a tree is like you?

When a slice of light slips under your
bedroom door at midnight, why is it fleeing?

If you remembered only one thing, would it
be that possum moms have 13 nipples?

Do you prefer globular blossoms like clover
or open-faced blooms like daisies?

When apples fall from trees in October,
do maple trees cheer?

Why does summer mist reveal ridges down
the valley clearer than bright light?

How many months can Joe Pie Weed
grow along riverbanks before it wilts?

Have you ever seen the golden dust made by
carpenter bees?

Will my tulip bulbs bloom if you plant them
three years from now?

Which appeals to you more,
the roots or the flowers?

What tale does an oak tell when its branches
rub together and squeal?

Does your dog snuffle or sigh
when she sleeps beside your feet?

Which do you think came first,
night crawlers or lightning bugs?

What does being alive mean
to a katsura tree?

If the beast can't be tamed,
why do we love music?

Is sunset you see reflecting off a city window
a real sunset?

Why are some leaves purple in the spring
and green in the fall?

What does a fish feel when it swims
close to a boat?

Is a chipmunk invasion evidence
of fewer owls and foxes?

What or who rules – the great abstractions of love,
beauty, and power or the invisible atoms
improv-dancing everywhere, all the time?

Why do we pay attention to the branches and not
the roots?

When people pitch nips and fast food bags out of
their cars, are they sick?

Is a scampering chipmunk really afraid
when a dog howls?

Does yellow live inside hosta leaves?

Would you agree a pile of lemon peels
and old socks is best left to rot?

If you left a PB&J sandwich on the lawn,
how long would it take the ants to devour it?

How many webs can a spider build
in one week?

Do forest birds in the same woods, except owls,
sleep at the same time?

Where do the brightest lights
on the planet shine at night?

Does a rotting deer carcass in the woods
smell like warm apple pie to bacteria?

When a dog barks, does it bother
the raccoons or chipmunks?

Does the color lavendar hide
under fallen birch leaves in the woods?

As the oceans rise, do the waves still crash
against Oregon bluffs?

What is the fragrance of a clear night sky
as it rolls over us?

Would we get lost if we used moss
on the north side of trees as a compass?

If curiosity killed the cat,
would sparrows and robins rejoice?

Will watching your breath tell you
how clean the air is?

How long until our molecules
return to the sea when we die?

How do bears find enough to eat?

What should we do if our sacred trees
become infested with scale?

Will sunset miss city lights
when they're gone?

Who flies away, clouds or us?

Why does the fragrance of rain splashed
on hot pavement make us happy?

Is the dark side as immense
as the light side?

When thunder rolls in the distance,
do birds know how far away?

What do roses smell like to bees?

Doesn't the autumn infinity of mushrooms
reveal the world is rotting?

Could the scent of millions of
blooming lilies bring peace to the world?

Why do so many deer sacrifice themselves
on Pennsylania mountain roads?

Will sunset miss cities when they're gone?

Does a little black squirrel's tussle
with a large gray squirrel lead to
squirrel sex play when she stops
at the base of the tree raising her
long black tail like a love banner
or are they only cousins or siblings
fooling around?

When a species of bananas dies out,
do they bury or cremate the trees?

If you listen carefully, when
will you hear a new nightbird's call?

When the loudest sound on the street
is a baby crying, do birds reply?

What is creativity?

Do hummingbirds ignore their feeders in August?

When muddy brown salamanders grow up
do they change colors?

What if a Golden Delicious apple tree
taught in high school classrooms?

Is inflammation the source
of our bodily ills or the symptom?

Have you noticed how fast mushrooms
sprout fruit then disappear?

Did you hear the one about the rose
that apologized for its thorns?

What can the mycorrhizae fungi on trees' roots teach
us about service?

Does the deepest part of the sea
wander from year to year?

Will humans ever evolve in reverse
to have gills?

Is anything unimaginable?

Where do bull elephant seals go
when they lose their last battles?

When dancers twirl, spread, leap,
does silence glow in their sweat?

Do elderly apple trees care more about their bark
or their fruit?

Will the night woods' insect music disappear
if we don't spray the hemlocks around the house?

Does death follow a schedule, only it's secret?

If fungus runs free from tree
to tree, why not we?

Is one vast wind composed of infinite tiny winds
dancing with each other?

Can people transform their personalities
in a radical way like frogs and butterflies
larvae to adult?

Do trees have their own names?

When in the fall does the forest perfume
smell sweetest and tangiest?

When October night mists rise is that the end
of bug-bite season?

Does thinking while walking
spoil the walk?

If a saguaro cactus spoke, could it tell us
the purpose of its life?

Will sunset miss cities when they're gone?

Does life make a mess
of natural order to cause evolution?

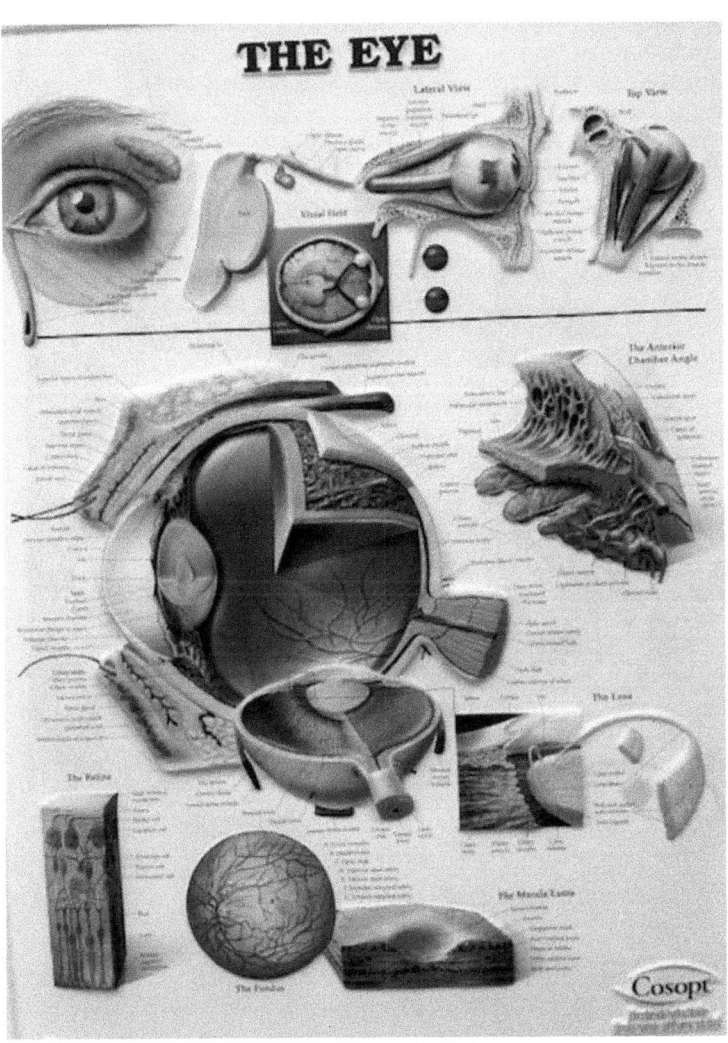

Society

S'up?

Are the names of babies becoming more exotic
or more common?

Who distracted the man on the motorcycle not
wearing his helmet?

Do long-lasting empty bellies
cause violence?

Was it right to plow under the wetlands to raise
up the solar panels?

If you log a forest, are you responsible to your
grandchildren for the lost oxygen?

What kind of world would it be if cars
stopped just so kids could play
in a sprinkler in the city street?

Are the people who build a skyscraper 150
stories tall jealous of basketball players?

Should we bury all the plastic bags in the core
of the earth?

If we're all one, who is all?

When you wear your mask, who is the outlaw, you or a bare-facer?

Where did the 3 million bodies go
after Columbus and his minions landed?

Why can't I cross the border when wheat and
soybeans can?

Do conference or Zoom calls let us
get to know each other better?

Does talent rub off or power or caring?

If you cultivated knotweed for tea,
would your neighbors sue you?

Is unbounded leisure the measure of wealth?

If you didn't believe in sin
could you know anyone who never sinned?

Figure 4.19

Who can you hear in the whistling wind?

Would people still go to work if they didn't
have to because the sky turned green?

Why do so few praise the works
of the pen unless they add up?

Would more people be happy
if they could ride the rain?

"Would you please come inside
unless you want to freeze out there?"

What if cars stopped just so kids could play
in a sprinkler in the city street?

Please consider my plea for help
and if not, tell me why?

How many years will have to pass before
white privilege to becomes all privilege?

Is the greatest power of the dead
their stories?

Would night rocking on the back porch
slow the growth of the stock market?

Did the ancient kings of Europe prefer
sour wine, fermented cider, or beer?

When someone mows their yard,
are they pretending they're settlers?

What can you do about the neighbor's house
they built too close to yours?

Remember when the U.S. Mail
brought news to think about?

Why do some architects design
Southern buildings for the North?

Is the state of Georgie overrun with asphalt
like it was overrun with cotton?

How alone can we be?

Who told you about me?

Is it true what they say about you?

Why do you ask?

Would you vote yes or no to raising property taxes to build the historical society a new building?

Are books promiscuous or polyamorous?

Is it the era of Covid now?

Is it mid-Covid?

Is it the late-Covid period?

Is Covid past?

Has Covid not reminded us of our weakness?

How many people do you know
who've been sick or died of Covid or any virus?

Do masks or denial work better for most people?

Are the heroes of Covid those who say
"Bring it on!" or are those the suckers?

When will we see our friends again?

How many safe pods can one person join?

How do we know if a pod is a safe pod?

Who's gained, who's lost weight?

Have we learned to wait or
are we just "Doin' our time"?

Do know more than one couple who's fallen
in love over the internet?

Are mirrors friendlier to us now
or do they avoid us?

Have you imagined the boredom they feel
in the debauchery pod?

Do you read eyes better now
that you've worn masks for a year?

Do you prefer plain or decorated masks?

Is it my vaccine or your vaccine
or their vaccine or our vaccine?

Do worriers worry more or less
after they've been infected and recovered?

Have churches and temples and mosques gained members or lost them through Zoom?

Will people rescue more dogs?

Do lacto-ovo-vegetarian libertarians eat eggs only from free range chickens?

Why the big deal in the business world about "disruption"?

Which countries does a blotto state of mind rule?

Did we waste so much water because we're mostly made of water?

Would a city window feel sad
if the fledgling hawks fly away?

Are sugar ants more loveable than lightning?

When someone asks for more,
are they hungry or lonely?

When would Jimmy of Jimmy's Produce on
Amsterdam and 83rd throw away
yesterday's strawberries?

When the poet Neruda rescued 2000 Chileans
from Franco, was that his greatest love poem?

When the great Lorca died, how does his
courageous spirit still live among us?

When the great Tate died, was his funeral
a laugh fest under a waterfall of tears?

How many years does it take for a country kid to
love living in Brooklyn?

When will the Golden Gate Bridge
carry only bicyclists and pedestrians?

Remember how outdated news was new
in the days of the Pony Express?

Where did all the pickle factories go?

When the optimistic athlete died,
was she cremated sunny side up?

Have you ever longed to smell
the metallic fragrance of the subway?

When will the government have to
subsidize sunscreen for everyone?

Is there a hierarchy of power in the land
of body lotions and perfumes?

How is white privilege different from racism?

Would we need heaven if everyone had what they
needed or is that Marxism?

Is it unconscionable that the rich people
don't take care of the poor?

If I proved whittling was the highest art
would you start planting trees?

Since neighbors are imperfect,
what do you expect from them?

Did you know, in previous times,
brown rice was famine food?

Where were the windows so smudged
sunlight turned gray?

What if the men called "Most Dangerous"
were the most competent?

Would you like to know why
human civilization was founded on sacrifice?

Wasn't it Jerry Lewis who said
"If it's funny it's got some sad in it"?

Will solitude evolve into crowdsourcing?

When someone says "Wasting time is good,"
why is that?

When people in chronic pain cry out
again and again, what do we do?

Was a name really the first spoken word?

Was a number the first written word?

Why do some people love their pets
most of all?

Is an atheist's prayer as effective
as a believer's?

Could the scent of millions of
blooming lilies bring peace to the world?

Is it a crime for an oak in the city
to drop acorns on people's heads?

If cell phones disappeared,
where would emojis live?

Is caring the most crucial aspect
of a job or the most challenging?

Is wearing a mask to prevent disease
anti-racist, loving, revolutionary, or art?

If a 75 year-old man believes in gnomes,
is he still sane?

Have you heard that more than 90% of
homes in the U.S. have air conditioning?

Is talking the most necessary act
for society to exist?

Are hunters more virtuous than farmers?

If we only walked and biked,
how much less asphalt would we use?

What are the three most important practices to
maintain a civil society?

When does repeating a word, a slogan, a phrase
become a crime, if ever?

In what world does a princess lose
her whole body but keep her powers?

How many animals watched you
when you walked to town today?

Who gives permission for anyone
to shoot anyone else?

Who quests in sandals?

If everyone ate and slept well,
would we be done with war?

Since money moves like a vapor,
will global warming cause it to evaporate?

Are today's repaired streets smoother
than the originals once were?

What percent of people will want
to own robots to cook their meals?

When will we free ourselves
from being slaves and slave owners?

When people wear masks and look
into your eyes, do you feel their love?

For how long will bloodlust
dominate the headlines about politics?

Would a refrigerator museum
enliven an old city downtown?

How can black and white piano keys
reveal the secrets of sin and survival?

How can the world's booming cites
relieve us of our ancient longings?

What does Covid-19 prepare us for?

Is the luckiest thing about working from home
you can kiss your mate anytime?

Shall we admire the homeless
for their lack of possessions?

Is fire our best friend
and our most fearsome enemy?

Are these the days when we all need
to be prepared for fire and ice?

Can we convert simmering hate
to evaporating bubbles of discomfort?

Would you want to live where
black bears prowl the neighborhood?

Can you imagine a society that needs no police?

Did you know that meat processing is the most dangerous job in the world for all humans and animals?

When we're older, can we fall in love
despite our regrets?

Why don't descendants of American slaves
receive reparations as do the victims
of the Holocaust?

Do you long for or fear the boredom of flying
across the continent?

Does having so many guns around
cause us to buy more guns?

When are we not scavengers and snobs?

How many kinds of bowing are required?

What did Dylan mean when he sang
"If dogs run free, why not we?"

In the future, will we stop needing cars,
trains, buses, planes but still need ships?

Can money step up?

Should we live as journalists, anthropologists,
or gardeners?

How do words and products
create new desires?

Is whiskey still the painkiller today's
cowboys prefer?

Is it arrogant and irresponsible to feel
happy during times of general terror
and suffering?

If someone's not a social activist,
are they like, hermits?

Will it be possible in our lifetimes for the people
of Israel and Palestine to enjoy peace
and prosperity together?

Will you someday meet the dark-skinned
woman whose eyes see all as you walk past each
other on the woods trail at dusk?

Have we lived through the worst yet?

Can we offer you anything you don't already
want?

Can democrats and Confucians agree on
the meaning of human rights?

Will robots redeem humanity
from our ancient sin of slavery?

Where did the bodies go
after Columbus and his minions landed?

Which comedian wrote a book called
Is this anything??

How could a person live in the forest
if they were afraid of falling trees?

When a person is beautiful, successful,
capable, fun, would a brook trout notice?

Do you have any enemies?

Are you one of those rebels?

Who will empty those trash cans in the park?

And the perfect world —
where was that again?

Wanna play?

SOCIETY 73

Philosophy & Art

Once we start asking, can we ever stop?

Will peace reign when most people are happy with their lives?

Who can tell us if we have a calling?

Could you consider my plea and if not, tell me why?

If you could answer a question yes or no would that be enough for you?

If it's true an infinite number of universes exist, would you choose this one? Why?

Why would someone stop asking questions?

If no one knows the answer, is the question science or love?

When you die will you leave a mess or a mystery?

How complicated is it to wait?

When is it necessary to ask
why do you play?

When you ask silly questions and someone tells you they're profound, is that human nature?

If someone says "nonsense" to the most profound comment, what do they mean?

Why is playfulness more effective than self-regulation in changing our minds?

If now is now and all is all, is nothing nothing?

Is there a last time for anything?

Who is more loveable, the comedian or the tragedian?

Who is more powerful, the comedian or the tragedian?

Why don't we know we're rich even if we
don't have much money?

Would peace of mind require happiness first
or after?

Can the mind ever be peaceful?

Though some want more, some less, does it matter?

If I confess to racism is that not racist?

Amica, quo vadis?

Would you call the terror of the unknown
and the longing for goodness siblngs?

If you change your mind after you answer, what
does that say about the truth?

Does time pass too slowly, too fast, or not at all?

Does "What did you have for lunch yesterday?"
have a simple answer?

Forgive me for asking, but what was
the first question?

Is arriving anywhere an illusion?

Are there only mysteries upon mysteries
within mysteries?

Does life depend on the sun's falling
in love with the sea?

How does a question become "old"?

Is true freedom having a book to read any time,
any place?

Why do old men and young women
prefer to drive cherry red cars?

Where is the most fertile place for old people to
plant their hearts' seeds?

Does money ever worry it won't have enough?

Do jokes ever laugh at themselves?

Is asking question a habit, a practice,
an obsession?

Will homo sapiens ever leave their caves?

Do we have deserts because the master gardener
wanted to grow cactus?

What is the main difference between
a Southern building and a Northern building?

Did we miss the train to Paradise because we
couldn't read the timetable in Tamil?

What is a fake-true answer?

If the sitar slides and the guitar howls,
what does a violin do in an empty room?

Is the secret of secrets
the most important knowledge in the world?

Do good ideas wriggle around like larvae?

From bacteria to moonwalking to
this question, isn't Nature all?

If a novelist begins plotting from the end,
why don't her characters age backwards?

Do musicians have filaments for sound
inside their ears?

If all my beliefs disappear,
what will my mind contain?

Do dreams tell the truth?

Is the answer really contained
within the question?

Does asking questions keep us young?

Is it urgent to know
if Neanderthal people sang?

When somebody says, "It's soft as a cloud,"
does lightning laugh out loud?

What would happen if
we give up questioning?

What is more important to our future,
knowledge or ignorance?

Is "yes" the most important word?

Is "no" the most important word?

Is "maybe" the most important word?

If we controlled our brains' reactions,
who is "we"?

Is giving up the belief in sin
an admission of evil in the world?

Which is more beautiful, a casual hodge-
podge of blooms or orderly clusters?

If God is Love, who is Hate?

Is God a who, a what, a how, a where,
a when, or all or none of these?

Are questions about divinity
like signs in store windows?

How long can a word
stay lodged in the brain?

Is it because death is lonely that it never
stops inviting more to join the party?

If someone predicts something will occur in 15
years, who would believe it?

If what my mind has left in it is not-knowing,
how long will that last?

Did the teacher wonder what we mean
when we said "ok"?

When someone said "What's the use?"
what if they kept trying?

Do we create problems because
we think we can solve them?

When does slowing down mean
not slowing up?

Why would someone set a goal
they believe they can never reach?

Is the idea of mystery
dementia or wide awake awareness?

How much of what we know
do we need to forget?

Does doubt honor mystery
or diminish it?

If writing narrows experience,
why does reading expand it?

Is the world more beautiful
or more just?

Just over the peak of Mount Shasta,
do patient angels float?

Is now a good time to begin?
At the moment of death, where is now?

In what language do steel, glass and concrete
prophesy their ruin?

Does "whatever" ever happen?

When someone says "I don't know"
do they express the basic human truth?

Are all conscious beings united in the truths
we discover, then forget in our sleep?

Are wild pollinator gardens more beautiful than
potato fields in bloom?

Is it smarter to read science fiction
or ancient philosophy?

What do you mean by "smart"?

As we age, do we become
our natural selves or no selves at all?

When will we allow ourselves
to feel awe?

What time of year does the good lord
of comfort rule?

Why would a grown woman volunteer
to stay awake for 72 hours, if she could?

Can we let go belief in the divine go
if we're terrified?

She said she understood only metaphors.
Was she a genius?

Can dragons and angels fly together
in blue skies and thunderstorms?

Are clouds and forests siblings
or mates?

If, as the philosopher says, all life is
problem solving, are solutions little deaths?

If a poem doesn't sing, is it poetry?

If mom and home are slant rhymes,
what about bomb and poem?

Is the purpose of a question to organize
our minds for a split second?

Is "What?" the most common question?

Is "Why?" the deepest question?

Is "Who?" the origin of love?

Where does a question arise from?

Is "When?" an exhalation of time?

Is "If?" the basis of change?

If it goes on and on, are questions
the lyrics of time?

Is "Is?" alone ever a question?

Does "Are" fit like a pair of gloves or socks
or pants or earrings?

Is the seeker of answers an artist
or a scientist or a hungry farmer?

Is "To be or not to be"
a question you would ever ask?

What are the questions we dare not ask
because their answers are terrifying?

When is it necessary to ask
why do you play?

What are the questions we dare not ask
because the answers might terrify us?

Science

---

4 servings per container
Serving size 1 unit (113g)

Amount per serving
Calories 120

% Daily Value*

Total Fat 3.5g	4%
Saturated Fat 2.5g	13%
Trans Fat 0g	
Cholesterol 0mg	0%
Sodium 290mg	13%
Total Carbohydrate 23g	8%
Dietary Fiber 3g	11%
Total Sugars 15g	
Includes 14g Added Sugars	28%
Protein 2g	

Vit. D 0mcg 0% • Calcium 71mg 6%
Iron 1mg 6% • Potas. 183mg 4%

*The % Daily Value (DV) tells you how much a nutrient in a serving of food contributes to a daily diet. 2,000 calories a day is used for general nutrition advice.

INGREDIENTS: WAYFARE DAIRY FREE BASE (WATER, ORGANIC BUTTER BEANS, ORGANIC OATS), ORGANIC CANE SUGAR, ORGANIC COCOA POWDER (PROCESSED WITH ALKALI), ORGANIC COCONUT OIL, ORGANIC GUM ARABIC, SEA SALT, CULTURED DEXTROSE, SUNFLOWER LECITHIN, ORGANIC KONJAC ROOT POWDER, ORGANIC SUNFLOWER OIL, CALCIUM CITRATE, NATURAL FLAVOR, VITAMIN

Are those who fall asleep easily
lucky, insensitive, or just relaxed?

Why would anyone want to eat
raw tomatoes with Worcestershire sauce?

Will you leave your house empty
with the microwave plugged in?

Will somebody invent a ladder to the moon
made from microplastic?

Where is the darkest place
on the surface of the earth right now?

If it were always night would we go blind
or see clearer?

If we're all one, does that include
all energy and matter and the unknown?

Could the peaks of cumulus clouds
paint the colors of lightning?

If someone you adored lived only in the past,
would the rocks in your garden ache?

Could we control clouds
with our daydreams?

How is electricity not a natural resource?

How long will it be before we admit
our true faith is in technology?

Will people in the future call us Gatesians
 or Luddites?

Are sugars still the spawn of the devil
and butters the largesse of angels?

Have you heard of the most common disease
in the U.S., "Ambien deficiency"?

Why do dreams fade faster after a good
night's sleep?

Does human life depend more on what we eat
or what we breathe?

What did he mean when he said
bikes are so damned efficient?

Can you yawn and sneeze at the same time?

Do shoes come with a quota of steps they can take?

Is lava on earth the same age as the moon?

Can the taste of garlic open a window
in Rome?

Can earthworms climb the Rockies?

When humans transplant a brain into a machine,
will it still be called Artificial Intelligence?

Since drones can fly, why not a Persian rug?

How is it possible MyRadar app tells more truth
than a sworn eye witness?

Could anyone stop evolution?

Why didn't the lightning rod and surge protector
protect the lights in the barn from the lightning?

Will we ever learn
the language of clouds?

Is there a limit to experiments we'll try
before we must give up?

How would you describe the difference
between purple and green?

Why do some rhododendrons blossom
like crazy, others not all?

Did we invent talking or
did talking invent us?

Animal, vegetable, or mineral
(silicon included)?

If a cardinal sings in summertime dusk,
who listens?

Can it be proven that imagination
changes reality?

If the sky was green,
would the grass be blue?

Can we change anything
or does change happen on its own?

What is the sound of a dwindling
September brook?

Isn't the world mostly water and weeds?
What creatures live inside clouds?

Where is absolute silence possible?

What is "is" in
"It is what it is"?

Can human commitment to naming things
make us immortal?

How similar to scaling on a leaf
is the scaling of a business?

When do mirrors reveal the truth?

Why does the bantam rooster risk tangling
claws in the brahma bull?

How many hours of screen time
before the world around turns gray?

How far into the universe
do Earth's sparkling night lights reach?

For every species we lose, who or what gains
and how long does it take and . . .?

Does chaos froth and spray?

When we start something, are we
seeds, amoebas, or rainclouds?

Are rampant spiderwort roots helpful models of
survival and expansion?

If we couldn't touch each other again,
is our skin sensitive enough to remember the
last time we could?

Is "why" an outcry programmed
into the human DNA?

What are the facts of now?

If "sitting is the new smoking,"
does it cause cancer?

How do we know what the backs of our heads
look like?

When are we most awake?

How does hate rot the soft pipes
of our hearts?

Is proper gear the best solution
to bad weather?

Do we say we're "spirit in the flesh" because
the atoms of our body are mostly empty space?

Have you seen the picture of the mating lizards
holding each other in their mouths for days?

Is human nature more limited than mycorrhizal
fungi feeding forest roots?

Have you ever argued with smoke from a
campfire about the meaning of density?

When the hibiscus flowers fall,
does the plant blame the sun?

Why ask?

How often do you hear
"Why not?" and you say "Too easy"?

Can there be an infinite number of questions?

Is the greatest weakness of computers
that they only give answers?

Have you ever argued with smoke?

Self & Relationships

Are you the kind of person who knows when
an idea is worth stealing?

Do you believe in yourself like a squirrel believes
she knows where she buried the acorns?

When you want to stop but can't,
how do you keep going?

If you keep asking questions, will you love life
like a five-year old?

Were you surprised or saddened when nothing
was the same as before?

Will you get up early to see raindrops sparkling
in puddles of the street?

If you could answer a question yes or no
would that be enough for you?

When you have to push yourself to finish
does the perfume of a lilac help?

Why wouldn't everyone agree with
"You ain't seen nuthin' yet"?

In your dreams, are you more male than female
or both?

When a house speaks to you
what happens if you don't answer?

Would you give up your dreams
if you could give up your nightmares?

If you take a photo of a flower
will you look at it more than once?

Have you ever kissed a wise woman
or held hands with a dying grandfather?

If it was a sunny June morning,
why would you stay in bed till 10?

Can you bear thunder and lighting all around
you with rational fear?

If you were a painter living in Fiji,
what colors would be your favorites?

If you're panting with desire, does your body
feel electric, on fire, or in a whirlwind?

When I walk toward the forest mist
do I seek tenderness from the trees?

Is it grief that drives our hunger to own things?

When you first learned to add and subtract,
did you laugh or cry?

Who can live in the city without praising
blue sky and dark shadows?

Did you hear the stoop in Brooklyn ringing
with children's laughing?

If you went bald at 17, what color
would you paint your head?

When a deer looks you in the eye, would you moan?

When juicy gossip comes your way, who
will you share it with?

What?

What th'?

Is "Hold me" our purest love song?

What does "Love grows" mean?

Can you desire the luminous being who may
or may not be available at the end?

If I tell you the meaning of green eyes,
will you plant me a flaming wild wahoo bush?

Can "Thank you" mean
"You're hot stuff"?

Was your dear friend buried on a sunny day?

Is asking "Are you Ok?" enough if your best
friend can't stop weeping?

Is there anyone alive who's never prayed?

What does the girl on her bike feel
when she leans into downhill curves?

When the coyote looked spotted us,
did he trot or sprint away?

How much depends on the yellow pill next
to the half full glass of water beside the bed?

When a helper helps you, how much
can they help if you don't want their help?

I'm one to avoid physical pain
or treat it immediately. You?

What kind of person would ever feel glee
about a real doomsday?

Will you remind me tonight
about the game tomorrow?

If it's your only chance to be with your
beloved, would you picnic in the rain?

If everyone followed their own sense of time
would we be freer?

When friends move out of our lives
all of a sudden, does our skin feel tight?

Have you found the loves of your life,
lost them, or both?

How much does it hurt when you can't touch
the ones you love the most?

If it wasn't for love,
then why?

Does each of us have a calling,
or several, or none?

Who would give a wedding gift
of homemade garlic pickles?

Do best friends become
best friends at the same time?

Why do being gently touched and gently
touching make us feel holy?

Do as many people feel as lively
as they seem?

How does keeping it simple
miss the point?

If someone speaks to you from the heart,
can you hold back your tears?

Why would you plant a tree
if you don't know how?

Do laundromat romances last
beyond the drying cycle?

When the worst thing happens,
who holds you?

Is it glib to answer "What if?"
with "Why not?"

Does creativity need encouragement?

When people say, "We're paranoid optimists," what do they mean?

What does "owning" a pet mean?

How can we understand
how we misunderstand each other?

Would you rather start a conversation
or keep one going?

Do you love your beloveds more now
than before?

When people believe violence wins, even in small doses, what do they fear most?

Are any of your friends higher than you?

Are any of your friends lower than you?

Are any of your friends younger than you?

Are any of your friends older than you?

Why do we say "boys will be boys" but not "girls will be girls"?

What is that rumble in the background?

Why have many transferred the legacy of whippings from violence to faith?

Why do some people cherish their hate?

Why do most people cherish love?

If they say "Listen," what do they want you to do?

Do the colors of painted toenails reveal a person's true self?

18
The Law of Success

Success often leads to arrogance, and arrogance to failure.

How long is your list
of all of those you care about?

If someone interviewed you,
what would you want them to ask?

Have you ever touched the coldest place
in your lover's heart?

Who would you wait for outside in cold rain
without a coat or hat?

How difficult is it to apologize?

Is the self a jumble of shards
we patch together with our breath?

If one of your friends wouldn't stop
talking, what would you do?

Will the downpour let up when
you make new love to your old lover?

Do we need permission
to speak honestly?

Is "who's there?"
our most profound question?

Do you believe what matters most is whether we
help or hinder communication with each other?

Do our bodies' bloody hearts awaken us
to the feeling of you and me here now?

Is sadness masked by our masks
and happiness, too, or can we show it?

Why do some feel embarrassed by others' pain
while some feel sad and some feel happy?

If you think I'm better than you, why?

Does it take courage or foolhardiness
to pan for gold in hating hearts?

Would you prefer to marry
your soulmate or your playmate?

What's so fun about dinner and a movie?

Is the self, as a poet said, the only history?

How are the words "forgive"
and "revenge" related?

Does slick, smooth lake water taunt the wind?

If you have one, would you please
sing me the lyrics of your favorite song?

Want to take a walk?

How can we keep the x-ray vision of childhood?

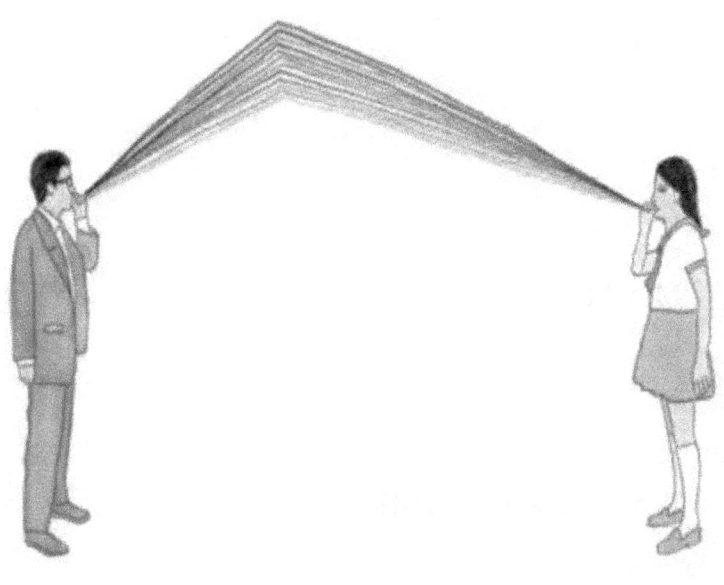

If 10% of people live in love and harmony, will they be able to move the 90% to join them?

I'm sorry. What was that?

May I help you?

Who wants to go first?

How do you tell the difference between a truth-teller and a liar?

If you don't profess a belief, can you still believe?

When a friend poses a question
and retrieves an answer
from a gray-bearded gas station attendant
watching engines waiting to be taken
apart and melted
and reassembled into guns or arrows
or computer cases or
artistically-designed porch railings
or molded pans used in hospitals
to catch blood
or in thick bottomed pots used in kitchens
to pop popcorn on Saturday nights,
would you agree almost
any answer he gives is correct?

Family

When a mother's prayers stop a tornado,
will her children laugh or cry?

Will the brilliant four-year-old poet
speak beautiful verse when he's twenty?

How is it possible to protect everyone
you love?

Can you remember your first sleepover
when you wanted to call home, but didn't?

When your parents die at 90, are you
an orphan or are you too old for that?

Where does the black puppy who came
to you in a dream live during the day?

Would you rather hear harp music
or silence or children laughing?

When she works late,
will you have dinner ready?

Can a loving father who lets his children
go their own ways feel truly sure?

When a mother's prayers stop a tornado,
will her children laugh or cry?

Will the brilliant four-year-old poet speak in
beautiful verse when he's twenty?

Why do brothers and sisters live so far away, even if
they're across town?

Mom, do I have to?

When the philosopher's son grew up
to become a sandwich maker, did she and her
husband cheer and clap?

Does "Bear's Den" sound like a good place
for a September boy scout camping trip?

Was it the favorite uncle who brought
the kids caramel chocolate chunky
ice cream telling them it was a gift
from the wizard who had no name?

If you were a parent, would you want your teen
to go off to a 100% safe, clean, caring, fun sex
camp to learn to be beautiful lovers and attract
and nurture love and happiness all their lives?

Can Grandpa ever find true love
when Grandma left him?

When will we stop listening
for Medivac helicopters?

Would you agree we should leave that pile of old diaries
to mold in the basement?

Does it confuse the old folks or the kids
when clouds scatter shadows then drag them back?

Why did the young man raised under the open sky
prefer the canyons of the city?

When your relatives come over,
do you hug them with all your might?

How much does who you are depend on your parents,
theirs, theirs & theirs?

Why do some grow up to be givers
and others takers?

When a brother is dying slowly,
who pays the motel bill?

Who are the ancestors
of the unshakably loyal?

Why did the children of the faithful
migrate when they didn't need to?

When a six-year old's energy makes
us happy, should we try to keep up?

Why are we like this?

Would you be a better friend
if you had no children, no parents,
no siblings, no cousins?

Which dreams of our parents
are we living every day?

Ain't we lucky?

What's for dinner?

Agency

How would a psychotherapist interpret
a dream about a venison dinner?

After reading a crime story into the night,
do you wonder why you woke up uneasy?

If they must wait two hours for the elevator,
will they want to go outside?

If you can't remember names of plants
would you still want to be a gardener?

Do you work harder than a fern works
when it waves in the breeze?

When you wait for me will you sit, stand, or
pace?

When you're closer to death than birth
would you still want to pierce your ears?

Will you stop your deep thinking
or at least laugh at my jokes?

If you gave up eating meat, would you feel victorious or
at a loss?

Walking the path toward the mist,
do I seek tenderness from the trees?

If your living room carpet could fly,
where would it take you?

When the door's locked and you've lost the key
who will you let climb in the window?

Would you take a dare to ride a police horse
across the Brooklyn Bridge?

What are three things can you not stop yourself
from doing?

If you didn't need money, would you work?

Is that house perched along the lakeside
waiting for me to move in?

When her majesty the hummingbird
appeared in the garden, did you bow?

Would you wear a mask in the meadow
to help bees make wildflower honey?

The Law of Failure

Failure is to be expected and accepted.

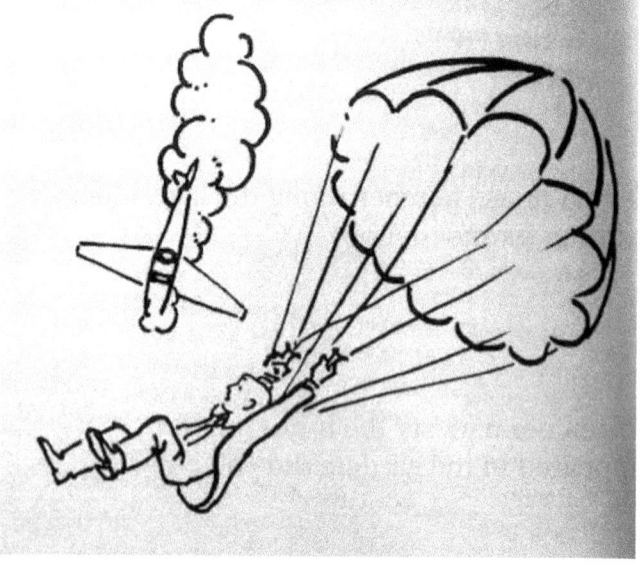

Who would carry a backpack filled with books
and snacks and a jump rope?

I want to ask you why but
will you give me a true answer?

Would you rather live in Alaska
or Ghana or in a place with no name?

Do you remember how to write
with a pen and paper?

Would you walk on a city street alone
on the night of the new moon?

Are you curious or fearless enough
to speak with beings of smoke?

How much work does it take
to cook a new veggie meal?

If you were already where you'd end up
would you make the trip anyway?

How many friends do you have
who still tell you you won't die?

When it became an ordeal to travel 50 miles,
how long did you stay home?

Where did all the money go or does it matter
after all?

Is it arrogant to not care what anyone says
about you?

Are you eating any new foods these days?

If the great achieved so much, why not we?

Is feeling more of a verb or a noun?

What does the boy think when he rides in
S-curves up and down the block?

If we don't stop now, will we be able to stop?

Did you ever want to ride in a Matchbox car?

Why do you work?

Do you ever long to smell
the metallic fragrance of the subway?

Which reveals your age more, never
wearing a mask or always riding an e-bike?

When the day brings no surprises
can you sleep well at night?

When do you stop caring
if you can't fall asleep?

If you really want to know
will you ask or will you try?

AGENCY 155

If someone asks you a question, when would
you reply with a question?

How often do you confuse the rumble
of thunder with the sound of a jetliner?

If you could control your dreams,
what colors would your clouds be?

Which territories does the blotto
state of mind govern?

Are there some questions whose answers are
too fearsome to ask?

Do you think more or feel more
when you take a walk?

Tomorrow, tomorrow, will I ask my fingers if
they'll learn to play the piano?

If my birthday snuck up on me,
would I be frightened?

Why do some of us do nothing for days
and others chug along no matter what?

When someone is angry is it due to feeling
fearful, belittled, justified, or?

If we don't believe in prophecy
how do we account for believing in love?

Is "once more with feeling" an insult
or an encouragement?

Do you prefer the uphill
or the downhill?

How much love is unavailable?

If you can't guess someone's intention,
do you run or pray?

Would you take a vacation
to dig up amber from a Baltic beach?

How often do you change your identity?

Will you remember more or less
of the rest of your life?

Is loneliness the root of most bad decisions?

Would you grow blueberries if you knew
birds would eat every single one?

Do you have the energy to follow your voctions?

Must we choose to eliminate our beliefs
or can we let them fade away?

For the latest news, do you watch clowns,
read graphic novels, or listen to birds?

If you could do the easiest work possible,
how long before you were bored?

If sexual desire doesn't end, is that a sign
humans might achieve immortality?

When you lounge in bed when
you could be partying, why?

Do you prefer the question
or the answer?

Do you prefer gazing at treetops swaying
or watching squirrels scamper?

Why do some nightmares linger for days?

It's getting late, isn't it?

Is it too late?

What will you do if you can't excavate
all the roots of weeds in your garden?

How do you know when your dreams mean
something you should pay attention to?

How does faith in the future
comfort us when we have a headache?

When you're older and love ever more,
how do you bear the loss of a love?

When you hear rumbling in the distance
do you feel curious or afraid?

If a doctor told you you were crazy
would you believe it?

Do crickets chirping keep you awake
or soothe you to sleep?

When the city is "blazing and boring"
how can you escape?

Do you remember your first memory?

When would you doubt easy answers?

If you lost your hearing, could you still hear
the lightest of breezes when branches moved?

Besides sight, which of your senses
do you use most?

If you're just starting out,
how close are you to the end?

When you've come to the end,
then what?

When does who we are matter more
than what we do?

What are your special powers?

If the world has more than enough abundance
to care for us all, why are we afraid?

Do you remember the feeling
of your greatest thrill?

How do you know if you have invisible helpers?

Does wisdom say things look good
so keep your eyes open and ears sharp?

Have you ever felt like or dealt like
a 19th century riverboat gambler?

When we learn we must drop old ideas
to grow, how do we decide what goes?

Without Zoom would I ask will I look younger
if I gain weight and lose my wrinkles?

Can your open heart feed your soul
and your body?

How much of our life
passes in the dark?

How much of our life
passes away in the light?

How difficult is it to always do right?

Why would you not bet
on a horse at a county fair?

When do we give up our fears of death?

If you were 14 now, what would you
and your friends do for fun?

Does it matter to you if you have to
play the fool to learn something?

If we believe deeply then learn we were wrong,
do we still hold our spoons the same?

What is an example of a life-long learner
changing her mind?

Who is this "I" everybody talks about?

Which songs would you memorize
to sing to your dying grandmother?

Do we forget so many good memories because,
deep down, we don't want to remember?

If we lose our longing,
do we lose our power to accomplish?

When a pistol fires, does a hum of loss
linger in the palm of the shooter?

What's skin color got to do with it?

Isn't our normal daily experience
an act of imagination?

Would you want to know the machines
that know you?

When is it better for us to love our superiors,
for our superiors to love us, for us to love each
other, or feel scorn, hate, grief, or humor, or
indifference for others?

Who wanders on foot and who rides
in autonomous cars?

Is "personal growth" humid and slow
like moss growth?

Does walking while thinking
improve the thinking?

If we come to a surprise crossroads
with five paths, how do we choose?

If we told the truth, would we say
everything is too complicated?

Are "yes" and "no" as promising
as "maybe"?

Does anyone really know what they need beyond
food, water, air, love?

Can kindness help us dance, even if we're flat
on our backs?

Is living a daily mess we spend our time
trying to clean up?

Is loving the best way to handle misery?

Is today the day we won't make a mistake?

Can we admit to fearlessness
because we've made it through the day?

Once you start it, is abandoning it
the only way you can get free of it?

Are the curious in danger
or are they the safest?

Who's looking for answers?

If someone told me "When you say something,
you say nothing" should I say anything?

Do like print books or e-books
or both?

When someone says to you, "My friend,"
do sounds disappear for an instant?

When someone says, "What's the difference?"
do you roll the dice?

If I say it matters,
does it?

Yes?

And now?

Question everything?

Do — what?

Be — who?

Do — how?

Be — free?

Do you have the energy
to follow your vocation?

Is it too early to celebrate?

Why do you ask?

When Whitman said "Nothing can happen
more beautiful than death",
what the heck did he mean?

Love

What is your favorite kind of love?

Do you prefer to give love or receive love?

How many kinds of love exist?

Does everything we do start
with love or loss of love?

When you "give your love away"
does that act increase your reservoir of love?

Have you heard of "biophilia",
the idea that life loves life?

Can there be any deeper purpose
than love of life?

Are all kinds of love "biological?"

When you tell someone you love them,
do you tremble?

When you love someone, do you have to trust them?

When you tell a group of people or animals you love
them, is that like ringing the dinner bell?

What are the colors of love?

Here is an incomplete list of kinds love:

Reciprocal loves - Mother, Father,
Brother, Sister, Friend,
Mate, Colleague, All living things,
Solitude, Play, Self, Spiritual, Art,
Thought, Energy, Creativity, Cooking.

Non-reciprocal loves: Work, Lust,
Power, Money, Control,
Empathy, Compassion, Protection.

Which kinds of love do you practice?

Which can't you do without?

Is love safe?

When a feeling of love becomes a habit,
is it still love?

Does the Quaker notion of "Brotherly Love"
include more than friends and family?

Why do some say hate is a form of love?

When your grandmother told you
"I could love you to death",
did she frighten you?

Is passion more dangerous than power?

When can fear transform into love?

When soldiers come home from war and lose
their minds, did they betray love or did love
betray them?

Can anyone say what love is?

Does acting from our hearts prove our love?

If love is the force that guides the good life,
why is the word itself so trite and vague?

Why are love songs the most popular?

If you love someone,
how much do you have to trust them?

Is virtual love real?

If you must do something, can you love it?

Why do some people love their pets
more than people?

When you feel love, can you feel the awe?

Does the song phrase "… it's a feeling,
o, it's a feeling …" describe only romantic love?

Is love too vast a subject
to grasp?

If you love me, can you hate me?

Where to all our lost loves go?

If "All we need is love", is that why
we eat, sleep, smile, grimace, dance, work?

If someone you love lies to you,
do you feel the shame?

Can love ever fulfil our longing for love?

Is longing for love
the longing for the unlimited?

Can we bear giving our true love to the world
with its suffering and random ways?

What is the difference
between empathy and compassion?

Isn't the first act of our lives
when two strange life forms join
to create a unique being
who is each of us?

Is love divine?

What would you do for love?

What does love forbid?

How many kinds of love
can one person feel?

Is love more a feeling
or an action?

How many languages of love exist?

Credits

Most of the images herein are random photos I took during my walks around town and from books, postcards, and internet surfing. I also borrowed images from artist friends and other artists. My thanks to them for prompting more questions and possible answers.

p 88   *Mask,* Andy Rothschild

p 144   *Sailing, Lake Merritt, Oakland,* CA, Danny Timmins

p 157   *Beached in Viaquez,* Wendy Foxmyn

P 169   *Circle of the Lustful,* William Blake

P 183   *Seven Sisters Sanctuary,* Goshen, MA

Thank You

Maureen Moore, my creative friend without whose quick mind and artistic vision could I have made this book?

David Grant, my lifetime friend without whose intelligience and patience and partnership could Zoetown Media be the unexpected nova at the center of my publishing life that it is?

To Amy Timmins, without whom?

When I look around, think about things, feel my way through the day, wonderings rise into my awareness.

Questions form. Answers sometimes come, more often they elude me. In the questioning, I discover nuance and mystery.

Asking makes me happy, with or without an answer. I wonder why?

Is it because, as I've heard, when we grow older our minds can become more open, more childlike, more aware that we're making our way through the unknown? With questions and answers our maps and landmarks?

When I wander the woods, I feel embraced by the life on the surface – standing trees and saplings, branches, leaves, needles, fallen decaying wood, ferns, wildflowers, mushrooms, insects, molds, lichen, animals and fish – and the hidden life underground – roots, tendrils, mushrooms, bacteria, unknowns.

Are questions the metaphors for the interrelated lives in the woods, how they nourish each other, how they are unified into one life form?

What do you, dear reader, feel and know about questions?

Books by Thomas Timmins
www.thomastimmins.com

Novels
- *The Hour Between One and Two (Trilogy)*
- *Blood Medicine*
- *The Special Fruit Company*
- *Down at the River*
- *Aphrodisiac for an Angel*
- *Subvocal (Illustrated)*

Short Fiction
- *Puff of Time*
- *Visions of My Other Self*
- *Desert Dusk Music*

Graphic Verse Novel
- *Zom*

Poetry
- *Likings for Shadows*
- *I Was Just Laughing*
- *Food Breaks Free*
- *Almost Everyone*
- *some say yes*
- *Never Been Here Before*
- *between worlds*
- *card tricks*
- *Questions?*

www.ingramcontent.com/pod-product-compliance
Lightning Source LLC
Chambersburg PA
CBHW071116160426
43196CB00013B/2584